School Work:
A Collection of Essays
on Improving
Facilities Management
in K12 Settings

Written By: Dan Ringo

School Work:

A Collection of Essays on Improving Facilities Management in K12 Settings

Written By: Dan Ringo

FOREWORD

What makes an organization succeed? Once this question is asked, it allows a significant improvement in analysis and evaluation of the areas that would need to be focused on. "School Work" is a book that is dedicated to helping K12 schools in improving the facilities management and helping them grow for the benefit of students and faculty both.

To begin with, K12 settings provide schools with improvised facilities to help improve student interaction, indulge in modernization and give schools the touch of excellence to operate effectively. This book will give an insight to improving certain aspects of the facilities to help attain significant growth in both the school structure as well as student life as well. K12 school facilities do not just excel at improving the infrastructure, but several other aspects such as staff development, master budgeting and so on. This book will talk about the details of how to work towards improving the environment and training the employees as well.

Keeping in mind that the key to growth of an organization lies in the satisfaction and hard work of the employees, this book will help you find just what you need to focus on for improvement.

FOREWORD

What makes an organization succeed? Once this question is asked, it allows a significant improvement in analysis and evaluation of the areas that would need to be focused on. "School Work" is a book that is dedicated to helping K12 schools in improving the facilities management and helping them grow for the benefit of students and faculty both.

To begin with, K12 settings provide schools with improvised facilities to help improve student interaction, indulge in modernization and give schools the touch of excellence to operate effectively. This book will give an insight to improving certain aspects of the facilities to help attain significant growth in both the school structure as well as student life as well. K12 school facilities do not just excel at improving the infrastructure, but several other aspects such as staff development, master budgeting and so on. This book will talk about the details of how to work towards improving the environment and training the employees as well.

Keeping in mind that the key to growth of an organization lies in the satisfaction and hard work of the employees, this book will help you find just what you need to focus on for improvement.

SCHOOL WORK

TABLE OF CONTENTS

Foreword

Chapter 1: Employee Uniforms

- Should They, or Should not They Be Implemented?
- Are Uniforms Good?
- Reference Links

Chapter 2: Employee Onboarding

- Why Employee Onboarding is Crucial
- How Will You Better the Process?
- Step 1: Make Sure Everyone Else Is Informed
- Step 2: Set Up the Work Space
- Step 3: The Orientation
- Step 4: The Lunch
- Step 5: Trainings
- Step 6: Being Up-To-Date

The Right Introduction

1. School District History

2. Population

3. Number of schools

4. Departments

5. Academic Calendar

6. Organizational Chart

7. Departmental Reports

8. Departmental Standard Operating Procedures

9. Completing a CMMS Request

10. Safety Plan and Importance

- Reference Links

Chapter 3: Training Calendar

- What is a Training Calendar?
- Creating the Perfect Calendar
- Types of Training
- Individualized training
- Interactive training
- Personal training
- Compliance Training
- Issues with Compliance Trainings
- How to Proceed?
- Reference Links

Chapter 4: Selecting a FM

- Understanding the Job of a Facility Manager
- What Qualifies A Person As An FM for a K-12 School?
- Defining the Right FM
- Differentiating Between a Good and a Great FM
- Evaluating a candidate
- Building the FM Report?
- Reference Links

Chapter 5: Selecting Quarterly Business Reviews

- Understanding QBRs
- Approaching QBR
- Strategizing QBRs

- Reference Links

Chapter 6: Selecting KPIs

- Bringing the Organization Forward
- How It Helps
- Using Competitions Brings Positive Results
- Reference Links

Chapter 7: Risk Management

- What Makes a Success Risk Management Program?
- Creating Risk Management Processes
- Identify the Risk
- Analyze and Evaluate the Rise
- Treating the Risk
- Keeping Track
- Focus on the much greater risks
- Focus on what effective training will offer a school faculty
- Focus on training early on—and take it seriously
- Final Thoughts
- Questions To Ask In Risk Management
- Ensuring Risk Management Is Given Top Priority
- Reference Links

Chapter 8: The Use of Committees

Chapter 9: Anticipation of Needs

- Reference Links

Chapter 10: The Importance of Disinfecting in the Workplace

Chapter 11: The True Costs of Deferred Maintenance and Poor Planning

Chapter 12: The Return on Investment from Making Quality Assurance and Benchmarking Part of your Process

CHAPTER 1: SCHOOL UNIFORMS

Schools have always had the debate of whether school uniforms are necessary. The debate has always gone in favor of having uniforms. However, when it comes to the school's facility employees, it is seen a differently. If there's anything that needs to be understood about Facilities Management it's how you will improve the way your organization is run, and the argument states; uniforms will bring a significant change.

In the case of school facility department employees, like other organizational members, implementing a change will come with a great deal of resistance. However, starting with something rather insignificant will go a long way. Employee uniforms are a great place to start.

Since the school is a reputable business, your decision on whether the employees should wear uniforms should ensure that it is taken for the benefit of the entire business. After all, a uniform help shape the public's perception of your operations as well as the employee's role and attitude about their job.

Uniforms in school's facility management focus heavily on custodial and maintenance employees. Because custodians are in direct contact with staff, students and stakeholders more than skilled trade personnel. Therefore, uniformed custodians will serve as identification to parents, teachers and school staff that this person belongs in the building

Should They, or Should They Not Be Implemented?

Let's move on to analyzing the benefits of implementing a uniform policy for facilities employees. Well, for starters, you will not have any issue in repeating where you work! However, for most people, it sounds like an extreme way of disregarding your wish to talk about the occupation.

So, what does the verdict say?

Well, it says that before deciding to implement a change that your best bet would be to evaluate your options thoroughly. After all, employee satisfaction is what will result in the improved performance, so you need to make sure that you're keeping their best interests at heart. Let's look at why they're commonly regarded in the positive light;

"The uniform makes for brotherhood, since when universally adopted it covers up all differences of class and country"- Robert Baden-Powell

First and foremost, embedding a uniform policy helps to give employees a little ownership for their work. Facilities employees with the same uniform attire tend to work together better. This increased cohesion tends to get the work done efficiently.

Uniforms invite organization inclusivity. This increased inclusivity allows employees to feel as though they are part of a team, which will bring a sense of pride for their work. A marketing professor, Victoria Seitz, from San Bernadino, California mentioned how uniforms tend to "entwine" employees to their company, ultimately resulting in success.

However, there's more to uniforms than just improved work. One of the things that uniforms tend to have is an effect of loyalty. Once the departmental branding and accompanying pride of belonging to something bigger than oneself settles in, employees tend to start to feel more at home. Teamwork brings organizational loyalty and creates a workforce which is more devoted to their company name, as opposed to with free and casual attire.

"But, what's the Downside?"

Completely contradicting the previous statement of an improved workforce; getting uniforms could also mean that there might be a chance of decreased work. How is that?

Well, most employees, if not all, might not be completely onboard with the idea, or even find the uniforms fit for their work. Apart from feeling like part of a team in some instances, employees may feel as if they are being discriminated against or segregated. a team, not against. In, certain schools where the employee groups are the only groups with uniforms, it might feel they are apart from the community, working in a subservient role.

Another problem may arise when the uniforms hinder the employee's ability to work and therefore diminishes the result. The material of the uniform. If it's clothing which is not suited for the weather, the discomfort brought about may significantly affect the employee's performance.

For example; a mechanic working in tight hot spaces may not fit well with nylon shirts and so on. Of course, these issues need to be thought of, and addressed, before implementing a change to properly manage it.

"It's Not Just a Uniform, It's a Representation Of Your Work"

The thing about employee uniforms is that they do not just affect the work; they tend to represent the person as they are, and where they work. Uniforms bring a professional image to light and allow the company to be recognized as a proper firm. In the case of school facility management, the uniforms play a major role in building a reputation.

Let's say, for example, you the decide to hold a bake sale for your school. If your wearing the school uniform, how well, or badly you do will be attached to your branding, or the company's name on the uniform. If the services provided deliver clear value, then the uniform has given potential customers a starting point to recognize you in the marketplace.

Have you ever noticed when you walk into an organization and you witness the difference between a person in a certain dress code or uniform, and a person in normal attire? The people in uniforms tend to give you, a consumer the satisfaction of being in a legitimate company, as opposed to the latter. Professionalism, in this sense, shows the expertise that the company holds and how confident it is to allow the outside witness their employees at work.

"What's the Downside?"

SCHOOL WORK

While most people hold respect for uniforms, some employees are not all too welcoming regarding their choice of work clothing being decided. Feedback may play a crucial role in distinguishing the likability of a company's reputation. In this case, if the uniform is seen to be disrespectful or distasteful in any way the organization might face unnecessary image damage.

The key to managing this issue is to ensure simplicity and add it to reflect the work that the faculty and staff members of the school normally do.

"Do not Scream Out Your Brand Name, Let Your Work do The Talking"

Advertisements are quite an important part of organizational growth, especially in the case of schools. However, why should you waste extra money on advertisements when you will do the work and have your attire advertise your company for you?

As mentioned before, if you hold a function such as a bake sale, you do not have to boast about your place of work because people would already see the name and initials on your uniform. Even a person simply passing through would see it and possibly show an interest. You're basically a walking billboard silently screaming out your organization's name, that is most effective when the results are clearly apparent from the services provided.

"What's the Downside?"

Well, if you do not do a good job at your work, or any extra- curricular you might be out for, you will still be representing your company. Any mishap will immediately produce a negative effect on your organization's name. This might also work in the company's favor since the employees will make a conscious effort to do a thorough and good job.

Are Uniforms Good?

At the end of the day, uniforms give you the authority to participate in shaping organizational worth and perception. Uniforms are a good initiative, but only if its employees see value in the brand and the subsequent pride that results. All the signs opt for a positive result with uniforms.

However, in order to decide, you will keep these considerations in mind;

You should determine the goal you wish to achieve through the employee's appearance, and rationale for which you're making employee uniforms. Would it be important for achieving specific results and impacting the learning environment? Are the uniformed employees providing an example that we want the students to learn from? Do FM service providers, or the academic staff and executives, feel more comfortable looking at uniformed facility employees? Addressing these questions openly and honestly will be able to give you a structured reason as to why you prefer making your employees wear uniforms. In the end, the goal should be a clean and neat appearance and the rest of the focus should be on the training received for performing tasks in a safe, productive and efficient manner in a respected, included and valued environment.

Is the uniform drawing the attention of 'fashion-conscious' employees? Because if it does, then self- consciousness will disrupt their performance. Individuality and self-expression should not normally disrupt the performance, but rather should be encouraged, to add to the value of an employee's work life. It is not uncommon for uniforms to be a symbol of control for independent minded employees, and this might result in resentment towards wearing it.

Some uniforms may encourage negative or rude feedback from parents or the general public. Service provider uniforms may draw the ire of an irate parent or community member, for conditions which are outside of their control.

Reference Links https://smallbusiness.chron.com/pros-cons-employee-uniforms-1741.html

CHAPTER 2: EMPLOYEE ONBOARDING

"THE GREATEST ASSET OF A COMPANY IS ITS PEOPLE." - JORGE PAULO LEMANN

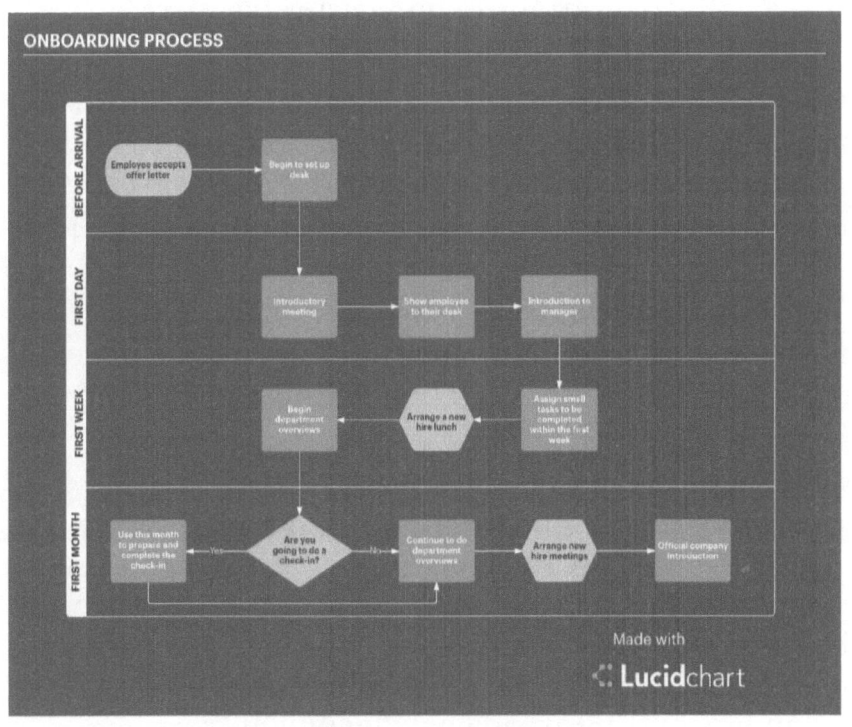

SCHOOL WORK

One of the things that every organization needs to pay close attention to is whether their employees are satisfied with the work and the environment. After all, it is the employees that tend to take your idea of what an organization needs to be and turn it into reality. In the case of school districts, you need to especially pay close attention to it because it is these employees who will then ensure that the school's community is run in an organized and appropriate fashion.

Lack of an organized role for new employees tends to have a dire effect on the students, as well as the staff's ability to learn and grow. The additional lack of resources, either human or financial, or the lack of understanding as to an effective onboarding process impacts a district's facility operations in immeasurable ways.

Because of this, it's important to pay close attention to how the employees are progressing, and what you will do as their employer to understand and improve their work. One of the most important things to investigate, however, is the very first step; i.e. the onboarding process.

It's crucial to ensure you cast a good impression of the department to new hires, since the first impression casts an overpowering effect to follow the employee's journey.

When making a hiring you need to make sure that you are fully prepared to receive the hire prior to their start date. Onboarding of instructional and non-instructional staff together for the components which affect every district employee takes great strides to emphasize the district's rules and regulations. Therefore, onboarding facility employees with others often creates a synergy and understanding among new facility hires.

In the case of K12 schools, the facilities operation program is built to provide clean, safe and healthy schools to help students reach their full potential. New hires must be ready to positively impact a school's operations the moment they are released to their assigned building. So, before we investigate the appropriate way to welcome an employee into the team, let's first consider why it's significant.

Why Employee Onboarding is Crucial

The first day, week and month of an employee's experience carries a lasting impression- Scott Weiss

So, what is it in the first place? Well, it's the initial stage of hiring where the employee is briefed about their responsibilities, the company, and all the relevant information about the work. It's a specialized introduction that officially welcomes the employee into the new team.

"But why is it considered to be so important?"

The process is important for several reasons, one of which is that it deposits into an employee an emphasis of their role and the importance that role plays in helping the district meet its organizational goals. It also helps to build the company's culture and boost the workforce accordingly. The top reasons why employee onboarding is important include:

IT INCREASES RETENTION

A study conducted by the Wynhurst Group in 2007 showed that a well conducted and organized onboarding process allowed about 58% chance of employees to stay in the company for more than three years.

The more a company retains its employees, the better the environment automatically becomes, allowing them to build a culture and increase productivity.

SCHOOL WORK

IT INCREASES ENGAGEMENT

Once the onboarding process is considered successful, it's seen that the likelihood of an employee engaging
with others increases. This proceeds to show an overall growth in loyalty and in productivity. The company
culture and environment is seen to be improved by the
input of an organized onboarding structure, especially
since the employee's perception of the workplace betters.

IT DECREASES RAMP-UP TIME

With a proper onboarding structure, it's seen that the
time for the employee to reach their maximum potential significantly reduces. This is because the employee is
welcomed in a way to make them feel more comfortable
and involved in the ways of the organization. Employees
arrive and to involved their assigned in the ways of the
location familiar with necessary processes and procedures to make an immediate and positive impact on the
school's operations.

How Will You Better The Process?

Well, since the process is better for both you and
your employee, it's important that you think about just
how you want to go about it. The secret to this is understanding just what you would expect from your employee. That would help you form an idea of what you want
them to know about your company. Once that is over you
will successfully move on to dictating what your process
will include.

Keep in mind that onboarding might sound like an
orientation, and while it's okay to consider it as an orientation, it doesn't necessarily involve paperwork and may
last up to a year. The key to excelling at the onboarding
process is to make sure that everything is taken care of

DAN RINGO

BEFORE the employee begins their first day. There are certain steps that will be followed in order to make sure the recruit is receives maximum comfort, and here are a few that you will investigate:

Step 1: Make Sure Everyone Else Is Informed

When designing the strategy of the right process, it's important to note that it is not just between the HR and the recruit; the process should also involve keeping the other employees up to date.

That means, on the day of the orientation, the team should be updated on the new member and how the team can make the new member more welcome. Once the team is are informed from before, they will be better able to assist the newcomer and help them through every aspect of work, from where they need to go and who they would be reporting to.

Remember, everyone is new when they join so it's always helpful to make sure employees use their experiences to help newer employees through similar confusions. It doesn't just help the employee feel welcome, but they will be able to communicate, understand, and feel more comfortable in the environment. Since the first impressions are what will carry them towards evolving accordingly, it's always better to present a friendly culture where everyone else is co-operative.

Just like a student's first day, the school's facilities management will work on this factor and train others to move ahead accordingly.

Step 2: Set Up the Work Space

Once everyone else is updated with the happenings around the organization, it helps to keep everything prepared beforehand. What does this mean?

SCHOOL WORK

Well, according to where the faculty will be hired, it's important that you prepare their workspace beforehand. Set up the computers, clean the area, and make sure everything that they might need on their first day is provided for them. In this case, they it would mean numbers for anyone who needs to be contacted in case of a problem, pencils, pens, and notepads which may be a necessity, passwords and links to sites which need to be accessed and access cards, if necessary.

One mistake that is commonly made is how emails and other the employee minor details are dismissed and set up in the last minute as the employee waits around. This will seem very unprofessional and give the employee the feeling that they are not necessarily an asset to the organization.

In order to prevent this, make sure to have a checklist of all the necessities and have it all up and ready to go before the first day begins. Every employer needs to also ensure that an employee's interests and items necessary for their work are available for them without any issues. A problem in the software or programs required for work will stall their performance.

Step 3: The Orientation

It's time for the employee to enter the premises. On the first day, set up a meeting with both the manager and the HR, and make sure that the employee is given a tour around the work space.

The meeting with the HR and the manager will introduce the employee to the organization and what the organizations main goal is. Once the relevant information is passed on, the employee will be introduced to their fellow colleagues, the relevant managers that they will be working under, and who they will head to in case of any questions.

This orientation will be the first part of the journey, which means every minor detail will have to be investigated and considered. This orientation will also lead to the employee meeting with the person in charge so they will be briefed about the responsibilities and how those responsibilities are normally handled.

Once that is done, sometime in the week, the employee will be given small tasks relevant to their specialty to give them an idea of what their work is usually associated with. These tasks will also help the employee's in-charge to evaluate how they work and move ahead with the information accordingly.

Step 4: The Lunch

Once the first day is successful, let's investigate how the first week will move ahead.

Apart from work, the employee is also supposed to get an insight into what else your organization has to offer. That means it's crucial that you plan out a great lunch to make them feel welcome and mingle with the other employees.

This step is crucial for the team to break the ice and get to know each other in a not-so-professional setting. No, do not plan a complete party, but even a small team gathering in the lunchroom will do the trick. The idea relates to how well the employee will get along with their fellow colleagues. This

interaction as well as the environment and allows everyone to offer their absolute best in their work.

A team lunch isn't to just necessary for the recruit, it also helps other team members to unwind, give them something new in the day, and allow them to better understand the people that they are working with. This social setting is an excellent unwinding opportunity for the managers to connect with their teammates as well. In order to help the organization grow, and avoid miscommunications

and unnecessary issues from occurring, a team lunch is the best way to grow.

Step 5: Trainings

What's crucial for the growth of the company is for the recruit to go through a series of trainings to help them give the best that they have to offer. This is regardless of whether they have worked on a similar project beforehand.

Every organization operates differently; and even if it's similar work, every organization has their own method of working. That is why this step is so important. No matter how experienced the recruit is, you need to make sure that they will use their experiences and better your organization's growth accordingly.

It's never too late to learn, and that is the motto that allows, employees to harbor their skills and modify them to compliment the current organization's requirements. Take, for example, a teacher. How they choose to teach in other schools may not necessarily be the same method used in the school they've recently joined. In this case, a training session would be required to take their prior skills and modify them to add to the method used now. This doesn't just better the teaching method, but it might also bring forward positive change in students.

Step 6: Being Up-To-Date

Finally, once all the other steps are done, make sure that a consistent evaluation takes place. Whether it weekly or monthly, or after a certain number of days, get an update from the employees and make sure their issues are resolved.

It helps if you're consistently up to date with their progress, so you know when and where the problem occurs. A consistent evaluation will help bring the employee to light, make them feel the importance of their work, and help them better their performance.

An evaluation also means that any problems that they might be facing is discussed in detail and then worked on how to move forward. This will connect the employee to the management and stay on track with what might be happening inside the organization. Evidently, this usually brings a positive impact and continues to help the employee feel like they are doing something that is worth the time.

The Right Introduction

The key to excelling at your school's onboarding process is to make sure that everything is taken care of BEFORE the employee is brought on board; that means before the first day.

For facility department members onboarding process should include a glossary and an organizational chart of the entire district including non-instructional and instructional personnel. Breakout meetings and specialized onboarding sessions will then focus on specific aspects.

During the time of onboarding, you need to make sure that the employee is aware of every aspect of your school. Keeping that in mind, here are a few topics you will introduce during Onboarding;

1. School District History During the onboarding process, discussing the school district history will allow the new employees to gain a much better insight as to where they're joining. The history paints a better picture on what to expect from the school, the kinds of students that attend the school, and who would be the best person to turn to in case of questions.

DAN RINGO

2. Population The population of the school will give the employee a rough idea of what their work will be and how they will be expected to tackle it. Introducing the population of the school is an effective way to give the new employee a sense of belonging. The population statistics told will include:

a. The number of staff working in the school

b. The number of students studying there

3. Number of schools

a. Classifications Introducing the school classification is a great way to let the new employee get an idea of what would be expected from them.

b. Specializations School specialization will allow your employees to get an idea of the work and how the school runs. Introducing a school's specialization is a great way to let them know the dos and do nots that is automatically required.

4. Departments The mistake that most schools make during onboarding is to only introduce the department in which the new employee will be working. At a school, everyone needs to be in line with the events of other departments as well in order to administer the best reputation for both the school as well as the students.

When introducing the employee to the school, make sure they are updated with all the departments, as well as the department heads.

5. Share the Academic Calendar The academic calendar shows how the school is run, the timing, and how much time is dedicated to which department. Most of the time employees are not informed of academic calendars and they end up making mishaps and losing enthusiasm for doing the work correctly.

In order to avoid this, it's always best to provide the calendar first-hand so any questions are immediately answered.

6. Organizational Chart An organizational chart gives a detailed structure of the organization; how the work is distributed, information processing and management control. This shows just how organized the management is, and just how well the progresses are reported. Make sure you keep these two charts in the loop as well:

a. Instructional (and)

b. Non-Instructional

7. Departmental Reports Consistently keeping track of the reports will encourage your employees to perform their best and provide the results. Make sure the meetings are continuously made in order to keep the employee in the loop of how their department is moving ahead.

8. Departmental Standard Operating Procedures These procedures are made to aid employees in carrying out the most complex work much more efficiently, and to allow employees to work better. Providing them with and updated departmental SOPs allows for maximum performance and decreases the chance of miscommu-

nication.

9. Completing a CMMS Request Make sure the new employees immediately have their Computerized Management Maintenance System logins and pertinent information. Employees must be able to demonstrate a competency of this system before being released to their assigned work site, as understanding and managing the workflow and tracking of maintenance requests is a key component of their job.

10. Safety Plan and Importance How up-to-date is the school with safety measures, and why is it important? One of the main things that every school should input in their onboarding process is to make sure employees are updated with safety plans and safety goals of the district, along with the vision and mission of the Office of Risk Management.

These trainings allow them to be more informed about the precautions and how the school tackles their emergencies. It also allows them to feel like they're working in a more safe and secure environment.

All of these, and more, will relatively help new employees get an idea of the school and how it is run. It's also encouraged to have video presentations available for the new hire to get a visual representation of the school's education system.

One of the best ways to better the onboarding process is to ensure that current staff members will relate their experiences and aid in creating an effective method.

Reference Links: For more information on effective

onboarding, you will also follow this link:

- https://www.shrm.org/resourcesandtools/hr- topics/talent-acquisition/pages/new-employee- onboarding-guide.aspx

- https://www.trinet.com/hr-insights/blog/2016/7-steps- to-an-effective-onboarding-process

CHAPTER 3: TRAINING CALENDAR

Is your organization facing a significant lack of trained employees? If it is, then you might be at fault and not them.

The issue with most companies is that once they bring new faces onboard, they tend to neglect existing ones. How do you prevent new employees form picking up bad habits that existing employees have developed due to an absent training or enforced training program? Well, creating, implementing, and publishing a district wide training calendar forecast is the solution. This should be mandatory for school facilities departments simply because policies and regulations are often revised and updated, which if not complied with will result in liability to the district.

In order to minimize risk exposure from employing a severely undertrained facilities workforce you need to develop, implement and publicly publish an effective training calendar.

SCHOOL WORK

What is a Training Calendar?

A training calendar is an adjustment made to the workplace where their employees are given authority and privilege to assess their growth on both a professional and personal level.

A training calendar is one that marks the employee's trainings and continuously organization, well as allows them to engage in new ways with the organization, stay up to date with the compliance trainings, as well as allows every employee to grow and enhance their skill set.

But how does a training calendar help in facilitating the improvement of K12 schools?

It's quite easy; schools are the places where faculty members and staff need to continually stay on track and improve the way that they tend to work. This, in accordance, helps the improvement of the school structure and student's curricula.

It's quite beneficial for the organization simply because it helps in retaining the employees and improving the way that they tend to work. This, in turn, will help in improving the environment in which the organization operates, and allow for certain skills to be evenly spread out amongst all members.

So, if you believe that some employees lack in certain aspects, why not turn around and ask yourself whether it's your lack of control that might have caused a problem? After all, as the organization's facilities manager, you will be given the responsibility to aim and improve the assets that work for you.

It's seen by Facility Services providers that training programs act as the main reason for service distinction in the workplace. By providing a calendar which gives everyone the authority to document, manage, schedule and prepare the monthly, quarterly and annual calendar, it significantly impacts how well the organization is run.

Creating the Perfect Calendar

Before you go about creating a calendar to benefit your organization, ask yourself what you wish to achieve through it? Once you have an idea in mind, you will be able to better create a target of the areas which need to be addressed.

Next, you need to make sure whether you want the training to be carried out in a collaboratively, or if you want an individual and interactive method of training, which will be based on allowing every employee to get the equal amount of time and opportunity to attain the trainings.

In this case, both methods will be quite effective, but again, it depends on what type of training you are planning to give your employees.

One of the most effective methods of training is to give your employees the authority to manage the calendar according to their comfort. This will give them the authority to take ownership of their development. This method is often referred to in a group setting, so employees will build their strategy and take control of their own trainings.

Types of Training

In order to create the perfect calendar, you need to make sure you have your company's motives in mind. Picking out the type of training to go forward with will determine how far you will go. Here are some options you should keep clear:

Individualized training This is a type of training where an HR team or supervisor's group manages the system. The calendar for individualized training often focusses on building strategies to minimize the gap in skills and focus on compliance training.

Interactive training This training often works when the opportunities are equally available to all the employees. Here, the employees are encouraged to take up the training, which is available, in order to develop and enhance their skills as much as they possibly can.

Personal training The personal or the team training calendar is basically targeted to a group of people. These are the people who are normally in charge of ensuring both personal as well as professional development occurs amongst the employees.

Compliance Training Compliance and work skills

are the most essential parts of training which allow you and your employees to stay up to date with the policies. While it's a necessity, in some cases, it's also a legal requirement for management operations to take care of.

Issues with Compliance Trainings

While compliance training is crucial for every company, the issue starts in regards of making employees maintain their sheets and take the training. Every organization needs to consistently update their employees with compliance trainings, which is responsible for updating them on rules, policies and regulations as they are mixed with their everyday work. While this may be a part of the law in some settings, in others, you have the authority to provide a little leniency to it.

Most employees, however, believe that it's not quite necessary and that leads to quite a lot of slack from their end. This is usually why employers and HR are stressed on how creating a strategy and setting up a time for them. This ensures that every employee is given the training and are up-to-date with their organization's requirements.

How to Proceed?

In order to ensure the problem is tackled, it's important to make sure that the organization's employees are well updated with the upcoming trainings, what you will do is schedule days and share it on the employee's portal. This will significantly help in getting the point across on a larger platform.

SCHOOL WORK

Issues with slacking in training will be tackled by developing and implementing times and dates for the training. It's also seen to make a difference if certain incentives are presented for attending the training sessions.

The Training Calendar should be included in the district's FM report to the district officials and/or school board on a regular basis, along with hours per employee.

A training schedule should be created well before it's time and put up so employees plan out their work accordingly. In this case, it will help both you, and your employees to reach an understanding on what needs to be prioritized.

Once the topics, presenters, dates and times of the trainings are set up, the locations and attendees should be confirmed. It's also beneficial to invite individuals from outside the facility departments in order to learn what is being told.

Training calendars often target the how, what, when and why's of the organization and is typically created.

OCTOBER

Sun	Mon	Tue	Wed	Thur	Fri	Sat
1	2	3	4	5	6	7
8	9	10	11	12	13	14
15	16	17	18	19	20	21
22	23	24	25	26	27	28
29	30	31				

DAN RINGO

Reference Links:

- https://www.highspeedtraining.co.uk/hub/training- calendar/

- https://youtu.be/A8RWICqziS8

CHAPTER 4: SELECTING AN FM

When opting to select an FM, the decision will vary depending on where you're selecting the FM for. However, before going into the details, let's investigate what an FM is and what their basic requirements are.

Understanding the Job of a Facilities Manager

A facility manager is required to look after several different jobs including overlooking employee relationships, building efficient teams, competing ideas, etc. They mainly are involved in looking over how to take an organization ahead.

In the simplest terms, FM's are mainly macro thinkers, as well as consensus builders, and work to get the right results accomplished.

A facilities manager needs more than just professional experience to qualify in the field, they also need to have the ability to build great relations amongst employees, and have a sense of empathy as well. If you're going to be giving your company's future into the hands of a facility manager, you need to make sure that they will tackle any situation that might come their way.

Let's look at how you will select the right manager for your organization. It's important to note that hiring just anyone with a past managerial experience isn't enough; a facility manager needs to have experience in the field that your organization operates in. For instance, a school runs very differently than a corporate office. Hiring someone with experience in the latter will have a significant effect on the way that they will run, as compared to schools.

What Qualifies A Person As An FM for a K-12 School?

Well, there are quite a lot of qualities that you will focus on if you investigate selecting a school's FM. Suppose you're selecting someone for a school; in this case, the election will mainly depend on the primary role within the school district.

If their primary workplace will be at a school, then the specific breakout onboarding will speak more to regularity of reporting, style, and how to be successful in an individual school community.

One of the main things that should be considered in this case, is how the training session of the FM will take place. That often means that the district principal will meet with the FM and translate exactly what would be expected of them. This reflects on how well the school's onboarding process has taken place and how much of the school's duties have been told.

Keep in mind, the prior mentioned aspect is your duty and as the head, you need to make sure that the school's values and motives are clearly mentioned.

This is where the school's onboarding process, as mentioned in the previous chapter, comes into play. All of this must be prepared beforehand, and the FM should be informed before the progress occurs. Remember, every employee is faced with a very different environment before they start working in yours, which is why it's important to make sure that they are aware about what to expect before they start working in your school.

School principals of today are required to be tech savvy and business minded and have jobs which regard both academic growth as well as providing an environment which will provide that growth. Since it's a job too much for one man to handle, they need a partner, or a trusted advisor, who will loop them in with the facility operations and advise them on the safest and most efficient manner used to maximize the facilities.

That's why, an onsite FM is required to be proactive, engaged and aware of the physical plant operation and academic programs and missions. They need to be able to have a business minded perspective on seeking out new and improved methods of ensuring contiguous operations while maximizing the building's use and minimizing its risk to occupants.

DAN RINGO

Defining the Right FM

If you want to define the right FM, you need to know that they are quite visible in terms of productivity. In simpler terms, they are basically the school's politicians with effective greeting patterns with the staff and building personal, as well as professional relationships. FMs make the schedules in order to plan the repairs and go ahead with other planning accordingly without causing much interruptions in academics.

The main job of a Facilities manager is to ensure that the school is run properly and in an orderly fashion. This means that all the operations lead to improving the school's environment. Not just that, it should also offer a safe, clean and healthy environment for learning without coming in between the students and staff members.

However, when highlighting the key qualities of an FM, it's important to know what makes the crux of your business. While most FM's aren't regarded as economists, mathematicians, or CPAs, budgeting still marks the key factor of the job. They need to know the organization's key metrics and how to plan and prepare based on the data.

When defining the right FM, it's also important to note that a weekly report is continually filled out in order to keep the principal on inside in the review. This keeps the principal updated on what goes on inside the building, and places their trust in the FM.

As the person in charge of managing the operations and relations, you need to be very careful in selecting a person who has had experience in working as an FM in a school, rather than simply having the experience of an

FM. That means with relative experience, the right FM will understand the principal's requirements and vision in order to create the right technique and fulfill the requirements. With consistent updates being provided, they should also be able to attend meetings where staff concerns are presented to tackle the problems arising.

Essentially, when defining characteristics, it could be helpful to list down what you might need from a Facilities Manager.

While there are a few common qualities, such as a skilled and experienced maintenance person with a strong knowledge of industry standards for operational elements like energy efficiency, sustainability and construction, selecting the right FM will go much deeper than simply that.

The keynote is that if the FM fails to see the importance in attending staff meetings, academic functions and other work-related functions, then they might not be a good fit for the position. It is then up to the principal to demand that school districts send more qualified individuals to their school that have demonstrably presented their capabilities to this point, and a willingness to consistently perform at this level.

Differentiating Between a Good and a Great FM

Let's say that you found a candidate that ticked all the points on your list, would you consider hiring them?

DAN RINGO

Well, in circumstances like these, it's crucial for you to know who comes under the category of bringing you forward, and who will bring your company success. The issue with deciding on facility managers is that they are often interviewed by academic leaders which means that their questions tend to see whether the candidate is proactive. Arguments say that it also depends on the finances available now, and while they will impact the situation, it is not ideal since it will result in poorer planning, preparation, and finally poorer performance in the learning environment.

If you really want to know how you will differentiate between a good and a great FM, then here are some things you will look at:

Good facility managers will put fires out on a day to day basis and great ones will constantly be thinking about prevention. It's not uncommon to have issues arise, especially if you're a facility manager. However, the difference here is that great managers will stay updated with the entire team, while running a log of their work and clients. Instead of consistently putting out fires, they'll find ways to ensure the fire is never set again. They will ensure clarity when answering questions regarding their next major tasks, the resources spent, and how they will improve workflow.

At the end of the day, facility managers want to move from reactive to proactive mindsets.

SCHOOL WORK

Good facility managers will cross their fingers the next HVAC system doesn't go down, and great facility managers will already have a plan in place for when that happens. Issues tend to continuously rise, and a great FM will know precisely how to respond in such instances. An article read that about 80% of maintenance is unpreventable regardless of the preventative maintenance schedule. This is exactly why having an action plan in place beforehand is so crucial.

Good facility managers will have a team of technicians that they oversee, GREAT facility managers will allow their team to be autonomous and constantly strive to be better. At the end of the day the district's facility expert is a manager. They will be expected to manage a department, a team and an operation that will require good leadership skills. A lot of leadership is intuitive, but good instincts will be learned. Based on the current environment and the direction the organization sees itself going, what personality should your FM possess? Should they be generally easygoing? Or should they have an edge? Either one may work well in different situations, but flexibility is an especially valuable trait for successful school district FMs and/or providers. Facilities Management is a dynamic profession. Every day is different, and problems pop up without warning.

Evaluating a candidate

FM evaluation is an important topic which must be investigated properly. Evaluating FMs means that they should first be able to answer the questions in a controlled environment. But what type of questions?

Well, questions which require in depth knowledge

DAN RINGO

and experiences which allows the candidate to provide the hiring into committee an insight into their thinking about addressing the operations.

Oral interviews are a necessity and the FM interviewing should apply the Socratic method of inquiry; which means that the questions should lead to conversations, which confirms information, verifying the responses provided in a written form.

Questions should allow a candidate to demonstrate proficiency in the following topics. Someone with no experience in facilities but extensive overall management experience should be avoided. For school districts, the learning curve often is too large. Here are a few things you will tell by their answers:

Quick and Composed – Is the facility manager able to think on the go? This is necessary because the day to day activities will throw a variety of challenges. It's the duty of the FM to react quickly and effectively with minimal pressure to address the concern. Handling stressful situations is a crucial skill for the FM.

Good understanding of the premises & Numbers – every facility is different, and it is the manager's job to gain an understanding of the facility and gather all the information to make calculated decisions. The information includes costs, consumption patterns, expenses, budgets, & trends. Critical thinking along with an analytical approach goes a long way.

SCHOOL WORK

Process Oriented- A process oriented approach makes it easier & faster to deliver a product or service. Increased traceability, metrics & quicker decision making are natural outcomes.

People & Vendor Management Skills - The FM is required to manage his people & also many vendors to achieve the necessary services. Effective communication, good knowledge of the subject,

along with people skills, will motivate the team. The facility manager must actively engage with the staff to bring out the best performance.

Risk Management- Facility management is the pillar stone for several other functions and businesses. Managing & active mitigation of risk along with business continuity planning assures smooth operations, even in critical situations.

Eye for Detail - It's extremely important to have an eye for detail, which helps identify any item, process or services that could become a risk or an issue.

Building the FM Report?

Let's look at why it's important to pick out the FM who is perfect for the job. The wrong person tends to increase the risk exposure and demoralizes employees. Why?

Because it has been repeatedly found that inexperienced people in positions of scope become more concerned with the perception of operations running well, rather than establishing and enforcing well-run operations. Their mode is survival in a position they are not qualified to hold, rather than focusing all energies on executing the game plan developed and approved by the district based on the available resources.

Some school districts may hire based on impressive resumes which will be difficult to confirm or verify. Often professional facility managers will claim success or knowledge of operations solely from being near the action that took place while not being directly involved or responsible for the results.

Executive titles overseeing facilities operations included in their portfolio does not make a facility manager. Facility managers must possess the proven skill set and requisite knowledge to synthesize the systems required or existing to deliver the best results for the staff and students.

Because deferred maintenance and poor facility planning often is the cause, or leads to the biggest financial liability for districts, the decisions to effectively operate the buildings may best not be run under a traditional leadership structure. The district FM may be a position best placed under a state agency outside of the authority of the local board, or at least have some autonomy to dispense the duties of their office, no different than an Inspector General.

School districts face costly litigation or potential litigation every day because of the conditions of its facilities. The funds used to settle many of the cases that come from these cases derive straight from the district's general fund. There is a direct and immediate correlation between failure to identify, understand, mitigate, or remediate safety hazards or conditions, which will cause harm to others, and the lack of available funds to improve education. Who should a school district have in the district FM position? Should they invest in someone with the background to address these sure to exist issues, or hire someone else, then pay for expensive consultants to only investigate and report the words of those who already work for the district?

A district FM should provide a district facility report daily to the Superintendent with a dashboard on conditions including risk and outstanding risk amount, cost of remaining issues of significance, code violations, and cleanliness levels at each school. A weekly report for cabinet should be provided by this individual with a monthly report being provided to the school board and community.

Topics of the FM report should include:

(percent of)

% of schools not heating

% of schools not cooling

(amount of money)

$ in risk liabilities

$ in safety violations

% of completed work orders

% of completed emergency work orders

DAN RINGO

(amount in repairs such as)

Plumbing

Electrical

HVAC

Carpentry

Roof leaks

(student attendance)

Number of meals

Money spent in meals

% of children transported

Reference Link https://www.quora.com/Why-would-you-hire-a-facilities-manager

CHAPTER 5: SELECTING QUARTERLY BUSINESS REVIEWS

Your school is an organization which runs on excelling its status by consistently improving its education system and environment. In order to do that, it's important for organizations as such to present forward the right Quarterly Business Reviews.

However, to effectively do that, it's important to know what QBR is.

Understanding QBRs

The Quarterly Business Review or Executive Business Review is a quarterly meeting with your customer in order to discuss their business and how you will be able to help them. They are important since they will report the objective of the services which are provided.

In definition, it's a basic meeting held just once per quarter with your client. According to SolarWinds MSP;

"It is a meeting with your client on a quarterly basis where you discuss their business and how you will support them."

Since it's a chance to allow your company's main stakeholders to analyze last quarter's results, they are then able to chart the progress for the upcoming quarter.

One of the most common mistakes that people tend to make is getting a tactical approach and bracing the customer's business with trainings and plan for improvement. However, the right way to plan is to offer them a strategy for growth.

A QBR meeting will also dictate the relationship between the vendor and the client. In case you notice a miscommunication or issues that consistently come up in between the meeting, then you need to consider working on improving your relationship first. Problems such as these will cause major conflicts and, instead of bettering the business, will diminish the results.

To prevent that from happening, the problems must be resolved offline so that it does not come in between the work. Turnover at the highest operational levels in large school district will be common. Failure of the operational staff to provide a recorded document such as a QBR leaves staff and vendors if outsourced scrambling when a new school or facilities leader comes in and asks for evidence of how well or how poorly facilities operations are performing.

Approaching QBR

Effectively going about a QBR meeting is crucial to ensure that you will achieve the most from the meeting. This isn't just beneficial for the school's growth, but also for the stakeholder as well.

One thing that you must keep in mind, make sure that you understand that the meeting is not a competition, both parties are working together to come up with a proper way to initiate progression.

Keep in mind that QBR meetings aren't often the place to plan additional trainings and further plans of improvement. It's a chance to better understanding of what the business is and how it operates.

Similarly, it's crucial to look at how you will ensure that more value is delivered. This switches roles from being the vendor to be the business advisor, thereby resulting in an improved relationship.

It's usually asked how to keep a QBR meeting. It's important to note that holding a meeting in person ensures that it meets the maximum goals. A face-to-face meeting is seen to be quite effective in the Customer Success Manager's toolbox.

If possible, the frequency and expected attendees for the QBR should be memorialized in the contract between district and supplier. QBRs are also an effective tool for in-house facilities departments. The KPIs remain the same and do not differ. There is no contract with a vendor so the attendees or audience would be different. The district FM should lead the QBR presentation for the department with the Superintendent, CFO, CHRO and a few board members fulfilling the role of customer.

If you're keeping an in-house QBR, then note that it should be very formal as well as allow members of the facilities team below the district FM to highlight their departmental achievements and provide some opportunities for professional growth.

Strategizing QBRs

In order to make sure you get the most from your QBR meeting, you need to know how to properly approach it. As mentioned before, you need to make sure that you build a good relationship with your client, which means that you should be able to use a tactical approach in your meeting.

Here are a few pointers which would be quite helpful for you:

Negate the Negative: It's important that you try to distance yourself from negative discussions; that means, try and focus the conversation on the successes instead. The customer should be able to give their honest input and grant you the opportunity to solve any issues that they may have come across.

Be Helpful: Most people tend to become defensive whenever clients put forward their challenges and queries. It's important to pay attention to the positive side and look for solutions to their problems instead.

Do not be Too Helpful: While it's important to look for solutions, it's equally important to know when you're going into overdrive. It's okay to preface your meeting by promising to handle those issues without taking up time in the executives' days.

Keep Time In Mind: Time is quite valuable and it's something that will help you earn the respect you need. Keep the meeting short and to the point. The meeting should always stay within the hour.

Remember, when you're leaving the meeting, make sure you schedule the next QBR then itself. It gives a positive effect on the client leaving them with an impression that says that you're willing to follow up. This way, you will easily expect results.

client, leaving them with an impression that says that you're willing to follow up. This way, you will easily expect results.

Reference Links https://www.gainsight.com/guides/ the-essential-guide-to- quarterly-business-reviews/

CHAPTER 6:
SELECTING KPIS

If you want to see the success of your company, you need to understand how to effectively select the KPIs. However, before going into the details, it's important to first build an understanding of what a KPI is.

The Key Performance Indicator gives the demonstration of how well your company will perform. You need to make sure that, as a facility manager, you will take your school to a whole new level and help it reach the optimum potential.

KPIs are essentially used to measure the organizations potential, and it's your job to make sure that you will cater to any flaws that might come in the way.

Bringing the Organization Forward

Understanding how you're opting to proceed with taking your company to a new level is quite necessary. There may be several tricks, but one thing that is seen to be the most beneficial for schools is competition.

It's always seen that 1 in 3 people will always be competitive and, of course, nobody likes to lose. Finding out the reason for winning is a must though. You either do it for bragging rights, or for tangible motivation, or simply to know that you will succeed.

It's no doubt that competition is quite healthy when

it comes to success, and once you add it to your facility operations, it brings a completely different edge to it.

Why, you ask?

Well, it's simple. Nobody likes routine, and by adding competition, it makes every day much more fun! Adding competition taps into an individual's socio-psychological need to understand self-worth. Both individual as well as collective pride will help tap into the mentality and bring about the motivational factors which allows for operation excellence.

If you have competition, then your performance automatically betters and the morale boosts of the involved employees.

However, when opting to add a little competition to your school, it's important that you manage it well and create an environment which is both friendly and involves inclusive competition.

Here's a great example for it; if you haven't witnessed a person participating in a 5k race simply because of their peers then you haven't witnessed anything! While working for a FM firm, it was seen that the boss had signed up for an annual morning 5k. Since he wasn't overweight, aged around 55 years old but smoked quite a lot, it wasn't an easy challenge. Yet, he completed in under 35 minutes which was pretty good.

While it did almost kill him, he admitted that it felt great. However, the only thing he could talk about was how everyone else in his age group and work performed. This meant that it mattered quite a lot how he was perceived to others and, along with him, it mattered to his peers as well. It was seen that these individuals had similar stories with the camaraderie of competition bonding them for the work they came to complete over the week.

But you're probably wondering what this had to do with facilities work, right? Well, it gives a significant insight as to how FM organizations will tap into their employee's competitive side. This is a major motivation that helps drive them to do better.

Most school districts often engage in something called "Fall Readiness" and it demonstrates how individual FM teams perform a deep cleaning of the entire building. This is all done to prepare for the arrival of fall.

It's traditionally a very heavy lift that employees, managers, and school district officials often dread. How do you get it done with less staff, vacations and summer school? Financial incentives could be one way if that is an affordable avenue. But how realistic is that option with reduced operational budgets year after year? The final question is how do you inspire people? How do you tap into that self-pride and protectionism of their colleagues to produce a desired result?

The answer is quite simple; create a Fall Readiness Program Competition among school buildings and managers. Before summer begins, sending a summary of the competition with a picture of the belt helps. There are discussions on how the teams will be updated and how often, as well as the cut-off date for the competition and where and when the results will be announced. Involving every stakeholder to raise awareness and garner interest and support for their own perspective is an excellent touch.

It helps when you take each building and divide it into sections weighted evenly except for classrooms.

Here's the division; most of a school building is comprised of classrooms. Hallways and stairwells were next. Cafeterias, gymnasiums and auditoriums were all weighted evenly. Then take the offices and lavatories together.

The rationale is that if a FM team completed 100% of all of the classrooms they would be approximately 65-70% complete with the building as the remaining items would not take as long as removing classroom furniture, washing desks and cabinets and dusting lighting and ledges before finally stripping and waxing the flooring and replacing furniture.

All the items were presented in an excel spreadsheet and placed next to all the buildings; the managers were expected to oversee and manage the resources were both on human (staffing levels) and capital (supplies/man-hours) levels to aggregately complete all their assigned buildings as quickly as possible.

Throughout the day, the Excel spreadsheet was updated periodically and sent over to the FM district officials once a week in the beginning of summer; preferably one week after the end of the school year in June.

The legend of the report was as follows:

• On-track is designated GREEN
• 1-5 days behind schedule is designated YELLOW

In the comments section FM provides "Action Plan" being taken to get the building back on track

DAN RINGO

• 6-10 days behind schedule is designated RED

In the comments section FM provides "Action Plan" being taken to get the building back on track.

Summer School or Extended year program could cause a facility to be RED

• Completed is designated BLUE

All buildings that are designated 95% or better

These buildings are requested by the FM to be visited by a senior operations manager and a district facility official to sign off on a BLUE designation.

The Summer Report should be divided into two sections: Maintenance and Custodial. The maintenance portion will have its own purview of topics such as:

• Percentage of lighting working

• Percentage of toilets working

• Percentage of water fountains working

• Percentage of sinks working

• Percentage of working stall doors

• Percentage of working exterior lighting

• Percentage of updated fire extinguishers

• Percentage of working clocks

• Percentage of boilers inspected by municipality authority (if applicable)

• Percentage of exhaust fans working

• Percentage of HVAC system working

This gives district officials such as a Chief Facilities Officer, Chief Operations Officer, Superintendent or

Board member, a high-level view of Fall readiness via the most current information available. August 1st of the Fall Readiness plans brings 2-3 day s a week of reporting. By August 1st, a summer school and extended day programs should have been completed. FMs will now further allocate resources to increase the intensity of the readiness and report over to the district.

District officials seem to become concerned with Fall Readiness when August arrives. It's not that they are not aware it is going on that during the last two weeks of June and July.

However, that they become immersed in Fall Readiness. District officials become laser focused on status updates and where the issues are to be completely done before teachers return for the fall.

How It Helps

The FM will stay in charge of the narrative of regarding all the aspects of the plan's reports when the updates are reported over to the district.

The Fall Readiness is a motivational and an innovative method to allow the staff to get the school ready without feeling like it's extra effort.

FMs are also able to communicate with the same way to the teams, and include who is in the lead and who has won. This practice began with a championship belt much like a champion prize fight, and the summary email in included a picture along with the mechanics and purpose of the competition. This was sent to all included principals and district officials.

The managers began to lightly taunt each other and talk about winning the title for the summer and being called "Champion" for the year. Each Friday when the end of the week results went out it was a part of the discussion the following week.

The competition is the priority in the employee's minds which meant that something special was hit. They see this as bigger than a paycheck. They see it as a team and a mission to get a project done and do their part.

Eventually, the program became a major success and had everyone to bring their all-time best to the project every day. When summer ended, the building for all the two weeks prior, without much difference in points. All teams felt accomplished and consistently stated that had never completed the Fall Readiness so soon in the summer.

An employee team party, which is not mandatory often regards the employees and their efforts. On top of that, since most competitions are completed early, the employees tend to enjoy a three-day Labor Day weekend. This is not common in facilities school operations in K-12 settings; however, it helps in bringing teamwork and motivation into the group.

Using Competitions Brings Positive Results

Competitions often show positive results when looking at FM teams and it is the FM's job to execute the competition parameters to disallow the discrediting of results.

It's important to note that the result should be excellence and support rather than winning. While winning may be the goal, if it's solely based on a competition structure without a learning process, it's simply not worth it.

Just as Fall Readiness came about, other competitions were responsible for engineers being able to complete work orders and prevent maintenance work orders. This is another way to recognize the high performers and competitions. FMs and Quality Assurance Scores, or principal visits, is another metric to create healthy oversight and accountability through competition.

As an FM leader, your goal is to find out how to motivate your teams to achieve and drive operational excellence. Everyone is not motivated by money, and oftentimes offering more money as an incentive is not an option. Recognition programs are great but highlight after events have occurred. Competition as an operational discipline manifests and monitors morale providing immediate feedback from beginning to the end of the project.

Reference Links https://www.quora.com/What-are-a-Facility-Manager-s-primary- KPIs

Chapter 7: Risk Management

If you run a school then you, of all people, understand just how many hazards there are in place. This isn't just the case for students, but also for the staff members and employees.

Risk management comes in as one of the most important factors to investigate when running a K-12 facility. It's not just about the traffic or the fire hazards, but also the labs and any emergency that might occur.

No matter the precautionary measures taken, there are several risk factors which might occur on a day to day basis. In order to make sure that both staff and students are safe, along with the school assets as well, it becomes necessary to make a proactive approach and mitigate risks in schools.

What Makes a Successful Risk Management Program?

SCHOOL WORK

Well, the key is to include a careful and planned strategy which helps take all the potential hazards into consideration. However, getting started is where the trouble occurs.

Most school districts fail to have a system which identifies the risks and the application of the process in order to assess them. This results in gaps in consistency for hazard remediation.

If you're looking for effective ways to manage risk and reduce the disruption of a student's education, damage to a school's reputation, loss of time, stress from incident management, and potential risks of legal intervention, then it's time that you took this aspect seriously.

In order to help your school become a much better and safer place to study and work, it's time you took some initiatives. Firstly, it helps to carry out a few risk management processes that will help you out.

Creating Risk Management Processes

It's important to note that the more uninformed you are about the risks that might come your way, the more you're putting your school, students and staff in danger.

It's always important that you have a plan laid out beforehand. The best thing that you will do is carry out these processes:

• Identify the Risk It would be a great help if you turned towards making a list of all the potential threats that may occur within the school. Identifying the risks means you are evaluating everything that might be wrong with the structure of your building as well.

Once you have that done, it is beneficial to make a list and start to prioritize the most significant dangers that pose as a threat. Accordingly, you will move forward.

• Analyze and Evaluate the Risk Once you've made a list, it's crucial for you to take it one step at a time. Now most of the risks are hypothetical situations which have the least likelihood of occurring. These are also the risks which are the most dangerous.

In this case, you analyze which ones have the most potential of occurring and try to build a plan to prevent it.

• Treating the Risk While prevention is a great start, you must also question yourself on what to do if the risk occurs. In this case, you need to make sure that you have a plan laid out.

Remember fire drills that you used to have back in school? Well, this is much like that. Prevention and preparation in terms of risks tend to go together. It's important that you figure out how to go about it.

• Keeping Track Once the prevention and preparation

is well taken care of, your job isn't quite over. How do you make sure that the problem doesn't occur again?

Well, it's simple, you do this by making sure that regular maintenance occurs. Not only that, keep in mind to investigate why the occurred in the first place, and then go about taking care of it.

Risk management is ongoing practice which you, as an FM, need to pay close attention to. Consistently working and progressing the risk management is what defines your ability to handle the problems. Here are a few enhancements that you will make:

Focus on the much greater risks

Lawsuits form the biggest concern to a school's reputation, but schools will not operate under the pretense that litigation is going to happen.

However, keeping the legal processes aside, it's much more important to focus on the lives that are present on school property. The business must be carried on with the context of keeping the staff and students safe. Fear tends to diminish the effectiveness of risk management.

Administrators must also consider relevancy. In the private sector, risk management has a large seat at the table, whereas with school district's that is not always the case. Depending on priorities, some issues that play a vital role within the school some may not be relevant in the private sector. Identifying the relevance of issues often determines where and how money is spent in a school district. District-wide funding will be one of the biggest issues administrators face.

Districts encounter daily challenges to come up with the right resources available to train staff—especially when it comes to implementing technology. Administrators must make tough decisions when considering funding realities and the need for as much risk management coverage as possible. They need to maintain a balance when money is at stake, as they are only able to make decisions based on the amount of funds available to them.

Focus on effective training

In must ever risk a management major strategy, safety training for the staff must play a major role along with ensuring that the district complies on both a state as well as a federal level.

One of the main things that significantly reduces damage and accidents from occurring is training. Safety training has a trickle- down effect, and if provided at the appropriate level of training, administrators will see a significant effect in reduction of accidents, damage to buildings and costs overall.

Improving school safety and collaboration is an ongoing process which results in the success of schools. As compared to past problems, the issues that schools tend to face now are much more the staff different, which means that regular training and resourcing the staff will help in making a difference will allow them to understand how to handle various situations.

Let's take online databases such as Safe Schools Online Staff Training System as an example. In order to make sure that all employees are updated with risk management, school districts distribute quality training as an effective way to raise awareness on the issues and how to tackle them.

The digital database also serves as a proactive approach to training. Having an online database enables staff to train in school or at home and ensures that everyone has the necessary training to handle a situation before it occurs.

In the end, by deploying an online safety training system, the district is saving money and time and will be more proactive in handling issues.

Focus on training early—and take it seriously

Safety measures is something that no one really takes seriously. That's exactly why it's important to keep the problem as the first thing to investigate and make sure that everyone is in line with the consequences.

It starts with everyone in the school district, from administrators and the school board to principals, teachers, grounds staff and even students. Everyone needs to think of safety and practice mutual accountability within the school community.

Final Thoughts

Risk management is something that is amongst the bottom of the management services that need s

focusing on. However, for the sake of their staff and students, district-level administrators need to be on board with risk management and make it a priority.

In schools, educating students is the main concern, and risk management is secondary. But just like in a factory where posted signs read "safety first" or "safety is number one," our goal is to get schools to think of safety and its importance to the school in the same way they think of education.

1. Field trip policies

2. Athletic event policies

3. Lunchroom procedures

4. Laboratory policies

5. Housekeeping policies and procedures

6. Visitation and Visitor identification policies

7. Background check and employment application policies

8. Zero tolerance weapons, drugs, and violence policies

9. Maintenance and inspection guidelines and safety procedures

10. Protection against unauthorized entry during day and when closed

11. Fire drills

12. Storm drills

13. School violence policies

14. Assemblies

Questions To Ask In Risk Management

How do you know that something is wrong and how do you evaluate the extent of the problem? Well, here are a few questions that need to be asked immediately:

1. Who got hurt, and what was the nature of his/her injuries?

2. What was the injured person doing, exactly, when the accident occurred?

3. What other persons were involved, directly or indirectly, in the incident?

4. What were they doing, exactly, at the time of the accident?

5. What physical factors were involved, equipment missing, defective, not being used? Why?

6. Were job procedures being violated? By whom? How? Why?

In summary, these questions are designed to determine which factors existed, that if they were removed, would have prevented the accident. Your school district will use a specifically designed form to gather facts after an accident or injury. The goal of accurate accident investigation procedures is preventing future similar accidents and providing a basis for a claims investigator to begin handling other aspects of a claim.

There is a common misconception that since Educational Services (SIC Code 82)

".....are not required to keep OSHA injury and illness records...unless they are asked in writing to do so by OSHA, the Bureau of Labor Statistics, (BLS), or a state agency operating under the authority of OSHA..."

that record keeping will be discounted altogether. The "Exempt Industries" are only partially exempt. School, like other businesses, should develop some method for recording and tracking injuries even if they are only using employment records and three a summary or more employees sheet. OSHA still requires that any fatality, or if three or more employees are hospitalized, is reported to OSHA.

Ensuring Risk Management Is Given Top Priority

In order to make sure that risk management is given the priority, it is crucial that all new employees undergo a period of safety training in addition to any new employee orientation training that may take place. It doesn't just ensure goodwill on the employee's part, but also shows consistency in allowing old employees to undergo the training again. Statistics consistently show that new employees have the highest accident frequency rate. Management must provide new employee training concerning specific rules and hazards in the employee's department.

All training and safety meetings should be document-

ed including the topics discussed, employees in attendance, as well as concerns raised by employees during
the meeting. After each employee completes the new
employee orientation safety training, documentation
should go in the employee's personnel file.

In the K12 environment some areas that need special
attention regarding training include:
- Labs

- Chemicals in use
- Kilns and art tools
- Kitchens
- Sports facilities
- Traffic plans
- Fire drills
- Storm drills
- Computer use
- Media equipment use and safety

The purpose of safety and health inspections, either
informal or formal, is to identify and correct unsafe conditions and work practices before an injury occurs. The
goal is to make the necessary changes in the work environment and employee behavior through specific, me-
thodical reviews. Inspection procedures to identify conditions and work practices that lead to on conditions the
job relates accidents to and the physical illnesses environment environmental is essential. Identifying unsafe
conditions relates to the physical environmental hazards

that may be present in a school. These physical hazards have the potential to cause employee injury. Examples may include poor housekeeping in classrooms, hallways, storage closets or other areas requiring employees to step over or around debris while working.

Unsafe work practices address human behavior which will be influenced through effective training and follow up. An example of human behavior that may increase the potential for injury in schools would be an employee's tendency to use a classroom chair instead of a step ladder to access out of reach shelves or items.

A formal monthly review of safety activities in place at the operations should be performed. This review is simply a follow up to disseminate information gathered during meetings, and review accidents or safety issues which have occurred since the last review period. Additionally, special review activities should take place. These reviews related to specific hazards found at many job sites will be eliminated by the following steps:

Monthly safety reviews by the safety committee

Semi-annual reviews performed by FM Supervisors

Unannounced reviews or inspections performed by the safety administrator

It should be the goal of the self-inspection policies to maintain a safe work environment the entire year, not just when an inspector is scheduled to visit. An effective inspection program will create the atmosphere of "habitual safety."

Management should have brief discussions about

various safety topics during regularly scheduled department or staff meetings. These meetings will be accomplished as a group or on a one on one basis, and should be designed to inform employees of any changes in safety policies and procedures. Additionally, any new hazards, which are being introduced to the workplace, should be touched on during these meetings in advance of the changes. All meetings should be documented and submitted to the safety director for review.

A school's emergency first aid procedures will depend largely upon the size of the organization. OSHA requires that any organization which has forty or more employees at one workplace have a designated "first response individual". This individual must be certified in CPR and emergency first aid training. Smaller organizations may have designated procedures such as requiring a witness to an accident to contact local emergency authorities. All schools should have adequately stocked first aid kits to be used in the event of an injury. First aid kits may vary slightly depending upon the hazards in an operation.

A current industry trend is for public places to have in place Defibrillators that are used to revive individuals suffering from heart arrhythmia and some heart attacks. If a company decides to obtain an AED device, caution should be taken to make sure someone with training to use the device will always be onsite. The purchase of AED devices on school campuses are becoming more commonplace.

Chapter 8: The Use of Committees

a. Safety/Liability

Facilities Committee

Best Practices

Trends

Issues/Accolades

An Interdisciplinary Facilities Improvement (IFI) Committee will have a significant impact on your facility operations. The idea is that members suited better to solve of results different issues are achieved via inclusion. Bringing together members of different disciplines in an organization will be best suited to solve issues, as well as be proactive and consistent in its operations and drive excellence to levels not previously experienced.

IFI Commeting Meetings should be monthly and occur at the same date/time. This will give your committee the consistency it needs to be productive and gather feedback on new initiatives and programs. The committee and its members all should have roles and responsibilities resembling any board or group of professionals that expect to accomplish what it sets out, and be taken seriously.

A district or region wide Interdisciplinary Facilities Improvement Committee should have a minimum of one person from the following categories: district facility representative, company senior management, parent, principal, teacher, custodian, engineer, operations manager, and a representative from your major vendors, i.e., landscape or supplies vendor. Having these member groups represented will ensure that your planning and discussions include every intellectual perspective involved with providing comprehensive facility services.

The rationale and expectation of what each member will bring to the committee is described below. Proper selection of committee members is essential for the group to do its best work.

A district facility representative will bring the district's perspective along with an understanding of district policies and financial resources, and appetite to pursue committee initiatives. This member visits several buildings in their daily travels and will help sell or discuss developing programs with other groups in the field, including other principals.

A company senior management member's attendance such as the CEO, COO, Vice President and/or Director of Operations would denote the committee's importance, and approve attendance of the hourly employees. The senior management member would approach or posit possible solutions for the group with a global or industry wide perspective. They will also bear in mind contractual, legal and financial angles that will need to be considered before due diligence, development and implementation would proceed.

A parent will be a great advocate for the committee and bring a unique stakeholder perspective. They are the end-user, and buy-in from this classification will go a long way in understanding the opportunities and obstacles facing facilities.

A principal will bring a wider perspective to the committee. Principals on average have more experience than teachers and would be able to speak to the previous effectiveness of recommended programs. Principals, like parents on the committee will help advocate for initiatives brought forward for implementation. Having one of their colleagues with buy-in will help buffer natural skepticism. As programs are tweaked to perfection principals will help explain the process, rather than a knee-jerk reaction to be scrapped, rather working through the obstacles of new program implementation.

A teacher will bring the impact of operational changes to their ability to instruct or directly carry out the primary mission of the district. They will be able to tell you the impact that feeding kids breakfast in their classroom will have on the flow of their day and impact on instruction. The teacher will be able to tell you how escorting children to and from lavatories will impact on their schedule etc.

A custodian will bring the perspective of a team member that is responsible for executing most of the initiatives the committee will develop. Custodians on the committee should have years of experience and have worked in multiple settings to productively participate in discussions with the other member groups.

A building engineer is the residential technical expert for all building. The engineer, like the custodian, should have years of experience in multiple settings. The engineer also should be of the higher classification or possess certifications.

An operations manager will help provide input to the group from a frontline manager perspective. This group member's perspective will also help tie in best practices and work flows from other school buildings when developing and implementing programs.

A vendor representative will bring a fresh eyed perspective to the committee. The vendor is not an employee of the vendor or of the district. They do business in similar environments, and possibly could offer best practices occurring elsewhere, or how programs considered would impact their ability to serve the district.

Now we have covered who should be on the committee and why it is time to look at what roles these individuals will fill. The committee is led via a Chair and Co-Chair. Professional titles are invalid during the meetings. Every participant and their opinions are equal. There are five titles for committee members.

Committee positions and their responsibilities are as follows:

- Chair
- Stop meeting
- Start meeting
- Direct the flow of the meeting
- Members is preferably a district or the vendor senior management official

2. Co-Chair:
- Run the meeting in the absence of the Chair

- Member is preferably a district or the vendor senior management official
- Provide preliminary research to substantiate proceeding on proposals

3. Recording Secretary:
- Record all substantial notes and discuss on agenda items
- Send out notes of meeting to committee members
- Take roll-call

4. Corresponding Secretary:
- Read proposals
- Receive and read all suggestions/communications

5. Committee Members At-Large

So now you have the who, the why, and the what, let's look at the how the committee will conduct their business. The committee will have a set agenda. The agenda will include approximately 8-10 items that span both a backward and forward perspective on operations. A sample agenda could resemble the following:

- Meeting Open
- Roll -Call
- Update on Program Implementation
- Issues
- Trends
- Impact to the district
- Employee/End-User feedback to implementation and application
- New Items/Business

- What?
- Why?
- When?
- Where to Pilot?
- How?
- Cost to Implement
- Timeline to Implement
- Support needed to develop and implement?
- Benefit/Impact to the district
- Operational Calendar
- Training Calendar
- Good of the Committee
- Meeting Close

After the meeting open and cordial greetings and roll is taken, the Chair should dive right into a report from the Recording Secretary on program updates and efficiencies realized, any issues or trends noticed from implemented programs, as well as the impact to the district. Any feedback, and from who, should be discussed for any necessary modifications.

During New Business, the Secretary though the Chair, will present ideas for discussion. After the ideas are fully presented, the floor will open, and any committee member will either express support or opposition for the ideas with an explanation.

The committee will discuss trends and review Standard Operating Procedures before implementation and rollout. Best Practices should also be shared at the committee to solicit feedback and discuss the research presented and its impact on all aspects of the school operations.

Through the Facilities Committee suggestions are received. It is unquestioned that when employees feel heard they feel even more valued. Valued employees perform better, and results improve.

With an interdisciplinary facilities committee, operations will be best explained to end-users. This is not an atmosphere for "know- it-alls". The committee operates with a Chair and Co-Chair. Work titles are invalid and have no bearing in the meeting. Every participant and their opinions are equal. The Chair and Co-Chair take consensus for voting on items to pursue.

One example of a plan that would arise from the Facilities Committee would be the development and implementation of a Building Operations Plan (B.O.P.) format. A B.O.P. would consolidate facilities information into a document, which is easily accessible and periodically updatable for end-users. Things like pending major repairs, filter-sizes, motor and pump types as well as bell schedule, student count, and facility staffing levels etc. This information, when requested, is usually requested at the most inopportune time.

SCHOOL WORK

Plan in an electronic format accessible via a web-based app, will allow district officials and facility managers to login and answer questions before they are asked. Now how would a new IFI Committee begin to approach developing the format and retrieving the needed information complete? What information would be necessary, and which building employee would be best fit to gather, along with how would this plan be best used in applications?

Chapter 9:
Anticipation of
Needs

1. Anticipation of Needs

Know your client's business

Think as your client should and as they think

Anticipating needs to me is defined as listening to building principals, teachers and district facility officials to problem solve, program build and strategically plan toward a common business goal by aggressively identifying areas of opportunity to be of service before those services arise or even realized. Anticipating needs from an operations perspective requires your FM teams to remain mobile, engaged and aware of the building activities and programs it delivers to the community.

As President and CEO of a Facility Management firm, I see my #1 job as anticipating the needs of my colleagues and clients. In other words, "staying ahead." I expect every associate/employee to stay ahead of the end-user or clients and colleagues at their work locations. This is only achieved by creating a comprehensive culture of engagement and awareness. Facility managers and their teams must first view the services the client provides its customers through their eyes, but with the knowledge and competency they have as a facility professional.

It's mandatory to view our services through the eyes of the end- user. When firms make this an institutional practice, engaged and aware FM professionals achieve operational excellence and customers and colleagues feel valued and inspired to bring their best to the business.

Serving K-12 schools means you are in the business of educational support services. How far or how well will you drill your operations down to the end-user? Do you understand the culture of the building, management style of the principal and how the surrounding community utilizes the facility? How well are you utilizing current events and trends to help support the mission and vision of the school?

How do you support the educational mission if you are a facility professional at a specialty school, i.e., vocational school? What about a Science, Technology, Engineering and Mathematics school? What about a PreK-5 primary school? What about a high school? What about combination school such as a K-12 or K-8?

In a PreK-5 school it is important to be proactive with compliance of licensing for any PreK classrooms. Safety compliance and regulations for PreK rooms should be checked daily and repaired often. Compliance status should be reported to school district officials on a monthly basis, whether requested or not. Facility teams should stock up on items for immediate replacement if necessary. Proper cleaning supplies for sanitizing and disinfecting areas where small children lay and crawl and emphasizing that to the frontline team as a routine practice is important. Safe and operable playground equipment is key for PreK teachers and principals. Principals want to know that the areas are safe, attractive and ready to receive students. What items are new to the market that increase access for students and decrease chance of injury?

A principal of a vocational school will not be concerned with PreK licensing and playground equipment safety. However, the operability of the ventilation system will be high on their radar due to the taxing from dust and particulate matter of construction and repair shops. Filter replacement and preventative maintenance on support systems are also crucial to your ability to provide consistent and reliable services. Vocational schools are more likely to be used during after-hours and weekends by the district and community. The district expects the facility to be as inviting and purposeful during off-hours as it is during instruction.

There are only a few things that will cause FM teams more angst than not being aware or ready to provide services for events scheduled by the district or paid for by the community. FM teams will often claim the reason they were not prepared for an event in their facility is due to not being told of the event in the first place. However, at the moment, this does not help support your client and their needs. It is more than likely to cause embarrassment for your client with their stakeholders. FM teams must diligently take all steps to proactively and repeatedly communicate or inquire about the facility's needs.

When preparing for events, the ability to schedule and allocate resources, both human and capital, are key. Proper staffing and building protocol knowledge, including contact numbers of appropriate staff, are key.

SCHOOL WORK

Thinking as your client does is different than how you think. As a facility professional you are there as the facilities and/or technical expert. You are the trusted advisor. However, to do what is needed or in the best interest of the facility and thus the district, you must learn to think as your client does to preempt or be proactive. Facilities is a discipline.

Reference Links https://www.riskmanagement-monitor.com/prioritizing-risk- management-strategies-in-schools/

SafeSchools Online Staff Training System

http://www.osha.gov/recordkeeping/ppt.1/RK1exempttable.html

Chapter 10:
The Importance of Disinfection In the Workplace

Sanitizing simply reduces the presence and growth of disease-causing microbes, rather than killing them. It is better than cleaning alone, especially in food preparation and consumption areas, but only reduces bacteria and does nothing to destroy viruses and fungi. To kill bacteria, viruses, and fungi, disinfection must be done on a regular basis. With proper disinfection, resulting in the killing of pathogens, the spread of office illness can be reduced or stopped altogether.

Handwashing is a great start in the effort to control the transmission of microbes in the workplace environment. Workers should be encouraged to thoroughly wash their hands with warm water and soap for at least 15 seconds following every restroom visit, prior to preparing food, and after contact with the public. Hands should be dried with disposable paper towels. This will help to reduce the spread of disease from person to person and from high-touch surfaces, but you need disinfection to take it to the next level.

SCHOOL WORK

Microbes land on high-touch surfaces where they can linger for days or months waiting to infect the next person to touch that area. Bacteria and viruses are opportunistic, seeking a way into their host. Once they have that way in, colonization begins and the host becomes ill. In the workplace this reduces productivity and employee morale. Especially during cold and flu season, illness can spread like wildfire in the work environment.

In those who have compromised immune systems those same pathogens can quickly become dangerous or deadly. Perhaps the microbe has become resistant, a risk to even those with healthy immune systems. This is one of the many reasons; desks, countertops, and other work surfaces should be thoroughly disinfected on a regular basis. More than just keeping surfaces clean and free of infectious microbes, disinfection can literally save lives.

For this reason, it is increasingly important that work stations be wiped down with a solution containing bleach regularly to eliminate contagions. Prepackaged wipes may be used as long as the label states that they kill bacteria, viruses, and fungi. Apply the solution liberally to all countertops, tables and surfaces, paying special attention to the most-used surfaces. Keyboards can be cleaned with a prepackaged wipe or with a cotton swab dipped in the bleach solution to ensure all crevices are disinfected. Telephone handsets, earphones, and earbuds should also get special attention as they touch the skin of the user and can cause infections.

Another source of infectious microbes that deserves

special attention is the devices that have become so popular in the modern technological era. In fact they are said to harbor as many as 25,000 germs per square inch. Our cell phone goes everywhere with us and picks up contaminants along the way. Tablets and smartphones now populate conference room tables in meetings and networking events. One sneeze can turn your technology into a carrier for disease. By their very nature these devices require users to touch them, thereby transmitting microbes to the user.

To disinfect technology such as smart devices screen-cleaning wipes with isopropyl alcohol should be used to clean screens and other surfaces thoroughly and regularly. This is especially important when they have been exposed to people who exhibit signs of illness, such as coughing, sneezing, or running noses. People touch their faces as much as 600 times daily, on average. Imagine the microbes they could be picking up from a smartphone that hasn't been disinfected.

The dreaded breakroom can be another source of contagion, especially foodborne pathogens. With so many people using the same food preparation and storage equipment and the overall lack of routine cleaning of the space, the breakroom is rife with microbes. Takeout left in the refrigerator to become office experiments, improperly cooked foods, and uncleaned spills all contribute to the need for breakrooms to be disinfected on a regular schedule.

Though workers should be encouraged to eat in the breakroom, because people who eat at their desks are exposed to three times the bacteria of those who do not, that space should be disinfected frequently to ensure that it remains a safe place for workers to congregate and enjoy downtime.

The communal refrigerator should be emptied and thoroughly wiped down with a disinfecting solution each week. Any items past their expiration date and take-out meals should be disposed and the trash removed. The microwave should also be wiped down to remove any spills and splatters, and the carousel plate should be washed in hot soapy water. Any other appliances, such as coffeemakers and toasters, should also be wiped down.

Because workers congregate around the breakroom table it is very important that surface be disinfected several times a week as well. Identify any surfaces where people are likely to be touching with exposed skin. For instance, if the chairs have arms, those should get a disinfection as well.

In the beginning it may seem like a lot of extra work as neglected spaces are disinfected properly. Over time, as things settle into a routine process of disinfection, they will take less time and become part of the workplace processes. In fact, other workers will be more likely to pitch in as they enjoy the new clean and safe work environment.

The National Institute for Occupational Safety and Health reports that up to 17 million workdays are lost due to flu, leading to about $7 billion per year in sick days and lost workplace productivity. According to the Centers for Disease Control and Prevention an average of 23,000 people are killed each year due to just the flu alone. Not only does proper workplace disinfection save productivity and money, it saves the lives of workers by providing them a safe and healthy environment in which to work and thrive.

CHAPTER 11: THE TRUE COSTS OF DEFERRED MAINTENANCE AND POOR PLANNING

If it's not broken, don't fix it, right? Well not necessarily. Like a car, facilities need to undergo regular maintenance and upgrades to ensure they're always in peak working condition. Deferring maintenance and upgrades to another budget year or until they are absolutely necessary can result in higher costs in the long run. Not only that, deferred maintenance can leave you open to liability issues and also affect other systems.

When formulating a budget plan and balancing the cost and benefit of projects there is a temptation to make cuts in building maintenance and improvements. It can be seen as an easy way to save some cash that might cover shortfalls in other areas. The reality is that you're gambling that equipment won't need to be repaired or replaced. You may win for a while and become complacent, but eventually your luck will run out and you could end up having to pay for multiple major repairs or replacements that will decimate your budget for year to come.

Deferred maintenance on your buildings is estimated to result in more than $1 per square foot extra in utility bills, according to a US Department of Energy analysis. That adds up quickly and could easily outpace the cost of the original repairs. In the effort to save money for the company, systems become less energy efficient and will put an increasing strain on the utilities budget.

When budgets are tight, everyone is asked to do more with less. It may seem an easy fix to cut the maintenance staff and budget. Unfortunately, in that situation, a major repair or catastrophic failure could easily result in costly overtime or even more costly employee safety risks. Planning for proper maintenance requires an appropriate level of staffing and resources to efficiently deal with routine maintenance, but also any emergency repairs that may arise.

A building where the ventilation system has been neglected or a leak has been ignored can become a "sick building," causing increased employee sick days and medical costs. This will begin to impact the budget in higher costs to provide benefits to employees, decreased efficiency, and loss of employees. Not only that, it can have a profound effect on a company's reputation and ability to attract top talent. No one wants to be known as the company that allowed poor ventilation or black mold to make thousands of employees ill.

Often the effects of postponed maintenance spread

and begin to affect other systems. In fact, a neglected repair in one system can cause a catastrophe in another system or area. A faulty heating and cooling system does more than just make employees uncomfortable. A cooling failure can cause servers and computers to over-heat and fail. Not only does that mean a work stoppage, it could result in a permanent loss of data. A roof leak can flood buildings, destroying infrastructure, technology, paper files, and valuable furniture and artwork.

Imagine the cost of having to tear your building down to the skeleton and to rebuild it and replace all the furnishings. This could result from that leaking roof that was not repaired in time to avoid flooding. Or perhaps an electrical repair was put off resulting in a fire that damaged the building beyond repair. Catastrophes like these are often so cost prohibitive companies have difficulty recovering and the effects ripple through the company for years to come, if not destroying the company outright.

Something that may not be thought about in relation to deferred maintenance, especially when a particular project has been deferred for years, is how it will impact a company's reputation and ability to make a good first impression. Broken or outdated infrastructure and furnishings can immediately make the most modern of companies seem behind the times. Imagine having a potential client meeting after the client has a ride in a shuddering elevator.

What does that have to do with costs? Everything! A poor reputation and bad first impressions have an increasing impact on a company's ability to do business over time. If you cannot attract clients or business, and talented employees, your budget will begin to shrink and it will become even more difficult to make a profit.

DAN RINGO

A very real risk of deferred maintenance is that it leaves you open to paying fines to regulatory agencies or settlements for lawsuits. Are the cost savings really worth the possibility of failing an inspection? How would you feel if someone was physically harmed as a result of a postponed repair? The settlement of a lawsuit, and the legal costs, are likely to be many times the cost of having made the repair or performed the maintenance in the first place.

So what is the answer? Planned maintenance and prioritizing operational investments will reverse the compounding costs of neglect. Planning for maintenance and upgrades ensures that they get addressed in a timely fashion, before they become a costly catastrophic failure. Equipment and facilities that are well maintained work more efficiently and safer, thereby they are less likely to incur additional costs.

When budgets include an adequate allotment for planned maintenance, it's possible to set up a schedule of maintenance that ensures all equipment will receive preventative maintenance or upgrades on a routine basis. With careful planning, this can actually increase return on investment and decrease costs over time.

Sounds logical, but how do you make it happen. Well first you have to prioritize your planned maintenance projects. Make a list of the things that must be done, the things that need to be done but can wait for next year, and the things that would be nice to do if the money is available. See the sidebar for maintenance that should never be neglected. Once you have this list in hand, estimate the cost of the repairs that should be scheduled for the year and then add funds to deal with emergencies. You may need to fine tune it from year to year until you get a good idea of the usual costs.

SCHOOL WORK

So you're in the budget meeting and resistance is rampant. Everyone thinks it would be best to cut the facilities budget and you need to convince them that course would not be advisable. Hopefully you have done your research and planning ahead of time so you can convince your fellow managers and/or VPs that the possible costs of deferring maintenance are just too great. With this preparation you will be able to defend your budget lines and make a case for good facilities planning and the budget to ensure it.

Highlight the high costs of deferring maintenance to save money. Make sure they understand that the money you save now could end up costing the company so much more in the long run. Paint a picture of the budgetary impact of one or more of those neglected issues resulting in a catastrophic failure that must be addressed. Make sure to contrast the lower cost of maintenance with the higher cost of replacement if the equipment fails.

Point out the cost savings in energy and gas usage when equipment is performing at peak efficiency. Employee morale and safety also impacts future budgets by increasing the productivity and innovation of the company overall, and the ability to attract clients and top talent for years to come. What it comes down to is return on investment and ensuring leadership understands the power of that return to ensure a healthy facility going forward.

Expect that you may be required to defend this planned maintenance each year until it becomes part of the normal operating procedure. Buy-in from leadership should increase as they see a savings in overall costs and how much more problem-free the facilities become. It will become easier and easier to see that well-funded planned maintenance avoids the compounding (report-

edly as much as 7% per year) cost of deferred maintenance.

Once the cost savings begin to be realized you can begin to move up some of the items on your "nice to have
list," ensuring your facility is always state-of-the-art,
modern, and running well. All your hard work and planning will continue to pay huge dividends going forward.
Just keep an eye on the plan and make it happen.

CHAPTER 12:

THE RETURN ON INVESTMENT FROM MAKING QUALITY ASSURANCE AND BENCHMARKING PART OF YOUR PROCESS

Quality assurance and benchmarking? Don't they do that at the manufacturers? So why should you do regular quality assurance and benchmarking in your facility management operations? While it's true that the manufacturer does quality assurance and benchmarking, that is more focused on the quality and safety required for installation. The quality assurance and benchmarking you should do is focused on ensuring that you have the best possible equipment and that it is running at peak efficiency. Though it is one of the most overlooked aspects of the facility management plan, there are some very real benefits to instituting a regular and robust quality assurance and benchmarking schedule.

Putting the right quality assurance process in place allows you to identify performance issues before they become a major issue requiring valuable maintenance time and budget to correct. Assessing performance on a regular basis will give you a feel for how the equipment or process should normally function. This familiarity throughout all aspects of your operation will help to keep your equipment, systems, and processes running efficiently.

One of the effects of good quality management is cost savings over time. By identifying issues at the earlier stage you avoid catastrophic failures that come with a hefty price tag. Having to tweak a few settings or replace a part will cost a lot less than having to replace an entire piece of equipment. It will also save on time and work hours that can be put to use in more preventative maintenance. Regular evaluations of processes can result in streamlining for more efficient completion of tasks. In an era where facility management operations are constantly being asked to do more with less, this is a substantial benefit.

Not only will you reap a savings and time benefit, but you will also ensure a safer environment for all who use your facility. That leak in the ceiling could become a slip and fall hazard. Broken tile or concrete could cause someone to trip. A regular top to bottom inspection of wiring, mechanics, and infrastructure help to ensure hazards are repaired quickly and don't become more serious. A safe environment will protect employees and others who use your facility from injury and will reduce possible legal issues going forward.

If quality is important in the leadership levels, it will become important at all levels. Employees will begin to feel pride in the workplace and a desire to contribute to the overall cleanliness and effectiveness of the facility. If the facility is allowed to become dirty and neglected and equipment is allowed to become broken or obsolete, it affects morale and employee turnover. Good quality control procedures improve employer-employee relations, which also contributes to employee satisfaction and retention. If you're not constantly having to replace members of your facility management team, you can spend more time developing your existing team into an efficient and dedicated team.

In addition to equipment and process issues, it may also help to identify or prevent issues with personnel. Quality assurance reports will highlight where employees may be underperforming or where there is inadequate staffing. It can also give you opportunities to reward employees who perform well or consistently contribute to good reports.

Are you having to defend your budget against budget cuts every fiscal cycle? Would you rather be able to spend your budget without having to justify every penny? Instituting an effective quality management process will help you to anticipate costs proactively rather than constantly dealing with emergencies and the high costs that inevitably result. When your department cost-effectiveness and running at peak efficiency more value will be placed on your operation and how it contributes to the institution as a whole.

There are many ways to accomplish excellent quality assurance. It can be handled internally or by an externally by a third party, or even a blended approach. There are pros and cons inherent in either approach. You will need to weigh your options, needs, and the budget and time you have to dedicate and then use that to make an informed decision.

Done internally by employees, quality assurance is a good way for employees to learn all aspects of the operation and how they should function properly. It will also help them to see how each different area interacts with and contributes to the operation as a whole. It encourages ownership which fosters a greater dedication to the job that is being done. New employees can be added to the quality assurance inspections as part of the onboarding process. This will help them to learn about the facility as a whole and to bond with fellow employees. It is also a lower cost option

One of the drawbacks of the internal approach is that your personnel may be too busy with their regular day-to-day tasks to perform the inspections needed. Another issue is they may not want to give a coworker a low performance score or there may be too much subjectivity in their evaluations. A good set of objective guidelines for metrics can help to counteract that, though.

Done externally with a third party service you avoid the subjectivity and feelings of persecution that can result from asking employees to evaluate coworkers. This approach gives you a dedicated team of experts who are trained to spot issues and to evaluate on an objective scale. You get instant accountability and compliance from personnel who have specific training and the appropriate tools for the job.

With a third party approach, you do miss some of the benefits of having it done internally, such as ownership and learning. That can be offset by having someone from your internal team shadow the external team and learn from them. This is also the more costly option and may require some justification to prove its worth.

A quality assurance system that allows you to have employees handle some evaluations and a third party team handle others may be the ideal way to balance cost and to ensure the best return on your investment. No matter what you choose it is extremely important that you institute a good quality assurance procedure as soon as you can and ensure it becomes common practice and is done on a regularly scheduled basis.

Benchmarking is another often-neglected procedure that should become a regular part of your facility management operations. They say that imitation is the sincerest form of flattery and they are not wrong. This is why benchmarking your facility against the competition is so important to your facility management strategy. Comparing your operation and facility against your competitors on a regular basis is a great way to ensure you are performing well and that your equipment is state-of-the-art.

Benchmarking is another method to use in justifying your staff and budget. When you compare your operation to the operation of another operation that is performing exceptionally well does your operation seem to be underfunded? This may be a way to justify funds to make improvements and upgrades.

It can identify whether your building is under- or over-performing and result in improving building performance. It can also show you techniques that may have changed or improved over time that you can apply to your operation. It provides a basis on which to evaluate various industry standards and techniques. It's also an excellent means by which to evaluate whether your equipment and processes have become obsolete. Once you identify desirable upgrades or new equipment, you can work it into the next budget cycle as a planned expense.

As you can see, a robust regular plan for quality assurance evaluations and benchmarking can benefit your operation greatly. A little extra work, in the beginning, can pay off in increased efficiency in your operations, higher employee satisfaction and lower turnover, and lower costs of ownership. With such a high return on investment, this is a process you'll want to start as soon as possible.

www.ingramcontent.com/pod-product-compliance
Lightning Source LLC
Chambersburg PA
CBHW031245280526
45784CB00004B/1725